To:

From:

compassionate
LEADERSHIP

16 SIMPLE WAYS
to engage and inspire
your team at work

PAUL AXTELL

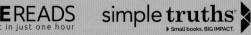

Published by Simple Truths, an imprint of Sourcebooks
P.O. Box 4410, Naperville, Illinois 60567-4410
(630) 961-3900
sourcebooks.com

Printed and bound in China.
OGP 10 9 8 7 6 5 4 3 2 1

I'm writing this book for every supervisor, project leader, or manager who wants to be wonderful to work for, who wants to create an environment where people can be themselves, at their best.

CONTENTS

Preface

I remember the first time I interviewed to become a supervisor. I flew from Seattle to interview for a job in New Jersey. After two days of learning about the job with the factory manager, Dave, we ended up in the hotel bar at about 11 p.m. I had already decided that this job and the notion of leaving Seattle for New Jersey weren't what I wanted. But then Dave said, "Paul, the truth is that you will have better opportunities than this one, but I need you, and the people in this factory need you. I hope you will give us a chance."

Most of us are drawn to people who are willing to be honest and vulnerable with us. We also want to contribute—to make a difference. I accepted, and I loved working for Dave.

Dave was sincere, authentic, and caring. He was also no-nonsense. I never worried about telling him the truth, probably because he always told me the truth.

There is an old saying: *People don't quit their job; they quit their boss.* If they can't physically leave, they check out mentally. It's just too difficult to keep working at your full potential for someone you don't respect or who doesn't seem to be on your side.

All of us, when we first think about becoming a supervisor, dream about being really wonderful. Then for many of us, that dream slips away or gets pushed into the background. Being a supervisor is tough. Let's just acknowledge that fact and get back to work on turning our dreams into reality.

It all begins with intention. The best people to work for are the ones who *want* to be great with people. Intention comes before skill building. Simply keep your intention alive and let it guide you. If you bring your intention to be a remarkable supervisor—along with a willingness to try and fail and try again—this book will show you how to make it happen.

**Let us all be the leaders
we wish we had.**

—SIMON SINEK, *LEADERS EAT LAST*

Lead with Compassion— The Perspective of Caring

> We have to choose to slow down, to actually see the time and space we are in...to truly see people and accept them in their priceless moments.
>
> —JODI HILLS, ARTIST AND WRITER

We can never know what people are dealing with in their private lives. People are often on the edge of some struggle. Life can be full of anxiety and stress and loneliness. According to a 2006 study by Duke University, people have fewer friends these days, and many people have no one with whom to talk when they need a confidant.

We, as leaders, should not expect to replace family and friends, but we can help fill the void. Work can be a place of comfort if supervisors lead with compassion.

People Need to Know You Care

I like the term *wholeheartedness*. It means you hold everyone in high regard, you see the best in people, and you recognize that everyone wants to be seen and treated as being unique and relevant.

You understand that people are complex and that their lives are complicated. You never presume to know how it is for anyone else, yet you want to get to know the people who work for you.

Caring means having people's backs, giving them the benefit of the doubt, and taking blame out of the equation.

You can be compassionate and still expect a lot from people—sometimes more than they see themselves as capable of doing. Being demanding and caring are not mutually exclusive; they complement each other.

My first supervisor, Kurt, was kind and easygoing. He had this mindset that if he hired you, he was responsible for you for the next twenty years, and he interacted with everyone from that point of view.

I'd been working for Kurt for about five weeks when he came in one late Friday afternoon and said, "Paul, I've been in fifteen meetings with you so far, and you haven't spoken yet. That's unacceptable. So starting Monday, if you don't speak twice during a meeting, at the end of the day, I will fire you. Have a nice weekend."

Then the following Monday morning, he said, "You know that what I said holds; you are on probation. You are the key engineer in most of these meetings, and if you don't speak, you've added no value. So start speaking, or I will let you go."

I rose to his expectations, and I took four lessons away from the experience. The first was obvious and immediate: if you don't speak in a meeting, you don't add value. The other lessons occurred over time:

→ Supervisors who care will tell you the truth, trusting that you can handle it.
→ We all have weaknesses that can be overcome.
→ Being nice in the short term isn't kind in the long term.

We all take lessons away from our teachers, coaches, and supervisors. The best leave us with more ability and capacity than when we first met them.

This book presents a range of tools that support you in becoming a supervisor who leads with compassion. In some ways, compassion is simple—it is caring. It's a trait we all have access to; we just need to pull it out of the background and into the foreground where it can shape our interactions with others.

You are reading this book, so your journey has already begun. Highlight the ideas and sentences that resonate with you. Look for things you can begin doing today. Each chapter ends with a suggestion about what you might put into practice. Here is the first.

The Compassionate Move

With respect to caring, what do you already know how to do that could make a difference to people working for you? Take a minute and write down five things you can do. Start there.

A human moment occurs anytime two or more people are together, paying attention to one another.

—EDWARD M. HALLOWELL, AMERICAN PSYCHIATRIST

Perspectives Change Everything, So Choose Empowering Ones

> When you change the way you look at things, the things you look at change.
>
> —WAYNE DYER, AMERICAN AUTHOR

I think it's possible to be good at whatever you choose—in fact, beyond good. You and I may not be freaky good, like Katherine Johnson, the gifted mathematician depicted in the movie *Hidden Figures*, whose calculations of orbital mechanics for NASA were critical to the success of the first and subsequent U.S. crewed spaceflights. We might not excel like Tiger Woods, winner of fifteen major golf championships, who put in thousands of hours of deliberate golf practice starting at age four. Still, we can improve every day and reach levels of performance and accomplishment beyond what we think we can. We simply decide that something matters, then put in the time to practice and improve.

A minor league baseball coach was asked what determines whether players get to the major leagues. He said that some players are naturally better, and they will make it to the majors based on their talent alone. For everyone else, it's not talent that sets you apart. It's these three traits: attitude, work ethic, and preparation. These are traits you can rely on in all matters of your life.

My favorite example of what you can achieve with the right attitude came from a Canadian veterinarian while discussing the idea of being remarkable. Ken offered this story:

One of my long-term clients asked me to come out to her ranch and put her favorite pony to sleep. She wanted to spend twenty minutes with her pony, then leave before I euthanized it. As she walked away, she turned and asked if I would also see to burying the pony. I said yes, even though I wasn't sure how I would get it done.

Later, as I stood in the field, I saw a church steeple in the distance and thought: church, cemetery, gravedigger. When I drove into the churchyard, an older gentleman stood next to a small backhoe. I explained my situation and asked if he would help. His response was telling: "I would be honored."

Two hours later, I told him the hole was deep enough. He replied, "Ken, you know your job. I know mine. This hole is not yet ready for her pony." He then spent another twenty minutes making sure the sides were perfect. He added hay to the bottom, then said, "Now it is ready."

Wow. Here is someone who has a remarkable attitude about his work—*I would be honored*—and whose actions match that approach to life.

Your attitude matters. Everything you say and do as a supervisor will be far more effective if your heart and mind are in the right place.

The first task is to create a collection of perspectives to remind you of who you want to be going forward. For example, when Cindy, my wife, and I travel, we try to follow this mantra: *If there is an experience in front of you, have it.* This perspective helps us step beyond our comfort zone and encourages us to walk down alleys to neighborhoods and cafés and bars we would otherwise have missed. This same perspective might be a useful guide as you read this book and start putting into practice the principles that may be outside your comfort zone.

Or consider this perspective from Mindy Hall, author of *Intentional Leadership*: *I want it to matter that we met.* Imagine how this might change the way you handle yourself in meetings, at coffee with colleagues, or during informal hallway conversations. Most of us pay little attention to how we interact with each other in the moment. Hall's perspective changes that.

Here are some perspectives to consider as a supervisor:

→ I care, and people know I care about them.
→ I'm going to be genuine.
→ I don't have to have all the answers.
→ I will always do the right thing.

Throughout the book, you'll also find perspectives to help with specific situations, like these:

→ It is a gift when people complain.
→ If I care, I'll have problems.

If I had to pick just one perspective to embrace, it would be this: *Treat everything in life as though it matters.* This doesn't mean that everything in life matters to the same degree. What this perspective means is that whatever you choose to spend your time on, you're all in.

The Compassionate Move

You are probably already results oriented. That's why you got the job—you know how to produce. For the next two weeks, choose a perspective that is relationship oriented. Try one of these:

▸   I want it to matter that we talked.

▸   I've got your back.

Then keep track of what you notice as a result.

Remember then that there is only one important time, and that time is now. The most important one is always the one you are with. And the most important thing is to do good for the one who is standing at your side... This is why we are here.

—JON J. MUTH, *THE THREE QUESTIONS*

→ I'M ON YOUR SIDE.

Imagine how work might be if you knew that everyone had your back—that they looked out for you and your reputation. You knew that if people had issues with you, they would come straight to you and not participate in gossip or undermining conversations with others.

More than your own success, you can earn credibility faster by supporting the success of the person sitting right next to you. Just think about the leverage you have when nine people on a ten-person team are worried more about one another's success than their own.

Now, imagine that everyone who works for you knows that you and their colleagues are on their side.

Never Walk Past Anyone, Ever

> For a leader, there is no trivial comment. Something you don't remember saying may have had a devastating impact on someone who looked to you for guidance and approval.
>
> —SUSAN SCOTT, *FIERCE CONVERSATIONS*

Kevin Kruse, host of *The LEADx Show*, interviewed me about how to conduct meetings with a focus on creating a quality experience for everyone who attends. Kevin began our interview with this question: "Can you tell me about a time you failed and what you learned from that experience?" I told this story.

Early in my career, I was transferred to a small factory in New Jersey to replace Emerson Eldridge, a supervisor who was retiring after forty years. Emerson was a gentle soul, respected and loved by the hourly workforce. In fact, he was godfather to twenty-seven of their kids.

A couple of weeks after I replaced Emerson, Dave, the factory manager, called me into his office. Standing outside were fifteen of my employees. I worked my way through the group, somehow sensing that I should not ask why they were standing around and not working.

The conversation with Dave is still vivid in my mind:

"Paul, you love baseball, don't you?"

"Yes."

"Well, when a team stops playing well, what do they do?"

"They fire the manager."

"Right. Why?"

"Because there is only one of them."

"Exactly. That's your team standing out there, and

they just asked me to fire you. You have an hour to convince them to change their minds."

I walked out of Dave's office, told the group what Dave had said, then asked what I needed to do to keep my job.

John, the unofficial spokesman of the group, said it simply: "You need to stop walking past us like we don't exist. We are people, and we want to be treated not only like people but like friends."

I got it. Not walking by people became a lifelong project for me.

We often forget that we matter to people, especially those we supervise. They notice when we don't listen. They take it personally when we walk past without saying hello or acknowledging their presence in some way. They notice when we don't ask for their input. If we ignore them often enough, they interpret our lack of interest as not caring. And if people think we don't care, we've dug a deep hole for ourselves. Think of it this way: there is a history of past interactions that frame each of our conversations. If the past pattern reflects caring, people listen and respond differently to everything you say and do than if they think you do not care about them.

It's also easy to take our relationships for granted, to be preoccupied or in a rush. Not everyone will have a boss like Kurt to impart this lesson in such an unforgettable way, so find your own way of remembering never to walk past people without acknowledging them.

Each Conversation Matters

Early in my career, I was far more interested in results than I was in creating lasting relationships. I didn't see the inherent connection between relationships and results. Only later, when I read Michael Nichols's book *The Lost Art of Listening*, one idea jumped off the pages at me: you don't change relationships by changing other people; you do it by changing yourself.

So I stopped giving advice. I learned to listen without being judgmental. I stopped talking about my interests and started asking others about theirs. I became thoughtful and determined to be focused on each conversation with my kids and my colleagues. I stopped doing just enough to get by or going through the motions. In short, I worked on myself.

People won't always let you know that your conversation with them made a difference. Trust me. It does. And each person you touch is like dropping a pebble into a calm pond, causing ripples out to other people in their lives.

The Compassionate Move

Slow down this week. Adopt an attitude that the conversation you are having right now is exactly how you should be spending your time. This person, this moment are what matter.

I'm convinced of this: Good done anywhere is good done everywhere. For a change, start by speaking to people rather than walking by them like they're stones that don't matter. As long as you're breathing, it's never too late to do some good.

—MAYA ANGELOU, AMERICAN POET

IF SOMEONE ASKS IF YOU'VE GOT A MINUTE, STOP.

Good conversation is like a dance—it's often easier when someone else leads and we follow. Take advantage of each opportunity that comes when someone else starts the conversation. Put the rest of the world on hold. Pay full attention. Don't interrupt. Let them finish.

Even if now is not the best time for you, stop anyway. If you do this often, your reputation for making time for folks will carry you through moments when you truly do not have time.

Trust and Respect Are Fragile but Essential

> You must trust and believe in people,
> or life becomes impossible.
>
> —ANTON CHEKHOV, RUSSIAN PLAYWRIGHT

Just as caring must be established before you can lead effectively, trust and respect are also fundamental.

Trust can be hard to achieve and messy, painful, and difficult to maintain. Even if we act in ways that inspire trust, there is no guarantee that people won't feel that we've erred. For some supervisors, the fragile nature of trust diminishes the effort to have it be a part of how they lead. However, the sense of personal integrity and fulfillment that comes with working on trust has extraordinary value.

I once had a manager who refused to allow other managers to interview me for another job in the organization. His explanation was that I was critical to a current project. I would have accepted and respected his decision had he been honest with me. But he did not tell me, and I found out later from another source. The relationship was never the same.

I love the following excerpt from *Letters to My Son* by Kent Nerburn because it highlights something most of us don't think about: if we do not act in a way that is consistent with what people consider the right way to do things, there will be a disconnect between us.

> *After laughter, look for a partner who deals with the world in a way you respect… If your partner treats people or the circumstances in a way you can't accept, you will inevitably come to grief… If you do not respect the way you each deal with the world around you, eventually the two of you will not respect each other.*

Trust and respect are mutually inclusive—you can't have one without the other. Many different elements go into creating and maintaining trust and respect. Unfortunately, like dominoes, if one element falls, the others often will also.

Here are some ways you can cultivate trust and respect:

→ Be honest, and answer questions truthfully.

→ Share information readily.

→ Be candid with people about their performance.

→ Notice who is on the outside and invite them in.

→ Listen with patience and complete attention.

→ Don't gossip. Defend those who are not present to defend themselves.

→ When you mess up, apologize.

→ Keep confidences.

→ Do the right thing even when no one is watching.

→ Don't blame anyone for anything.

→ Be kind, gracious, and courteous.

There are five broad principles that empower the preceding actions.

Be authentic. This is simple. Just be yourself. Say what you think. Mean what you say. Be candid, honest, and respectful. As long as you are sincere and responsible for what you say and how you say it, people will respect you for your openness.

Share more. My daughter, Amy, once called with a simple request. "Dad, you've got to share more." My preference is to be quiet. Yet relationships are kept vibrant with conversation, so my personal preferences don't matter. It's difficult to feel connected to or safe with someone who doesn't say much. Take the point of view that if someone invites you to speak, you are obligated to respond. Listen for those moments and find something to share.

Be less judgmental. Respect people as they are. You have probably met people with whom you feel instantly comfortable and at ease. It is often because of their ability to like and accept you as you are. The quickest and perhaps most reliable way to feel trust with another is to have the experience of being seen and understood for who you really are.

View vulnerability as a strength. People love underdogs, so you really can't go wrong sharing about when you messed up. Honesty can be painful, but it will be appreciated. Everyone can relate to your mistakes with one of their own.

View conflict as a sign of trust. Most of us were raised to avoid confrontation. Your most valuable colleagues and friends push back when you say or do something they don't see as right or useful. So relax a bit when the conversation in your group gets spirited. Invite different views and respectful disagreement. Trust that the group will come back to a good place. Because it will.

The Compassionate Move

Look at the eleven ways to cultivate trust and respect. Choose one and practice it for a week. Then next week, pick another one to practice.

Vulnerability sounds like truth and feels like courage. Truth and courage aren't always comfortable, but they're never weakness.

—BRENÉ BROWN, *THE POWER OF VULNERABILITY*

→ USE SIMPLE COURTESIES.

Years ago, my wife, Cindy, was telling me about Mike, a manager she said I had met. I couldn't put a face with the name, so she kept describing where we'd met and what we'd talked about.

Finally, she said, "Well, Mike might be about the most gracious person I've ever met."

"Gracious. What is that?"

"You wouldn't know."

Well, she was right, and for thirty years, Cindy has been pointing out to me examples of someone being gracious, such as not blaming anyone, taking right and wrong out of the conversation, letting people know what we appreciate about them, and being kind.

Another part of being gracious is to use simple courtesies like please and thank you. They don't take much, and they're an important addition to your social skills.

People Are Complicated— and Sometimes Difficult

> **"Sometimes people do things that are complicated. For complicated reasons."**
>
> **—LAUREN BARNHOLDT, *SOMETIMES IT HAPPENS***

I can still recall many pieces of wisdom that Robert Berra, one of my mentors, shared with me. This one has held up over time: "Paul, just remember one thing when you are in any circumstance where people are not being their best selves: *Everyone is a little bit scared and a whole lot proud.*"

I think this sentiment resonated because it described me. Growing up, I felt as if I was the only one who was scared. When I remember this statement,

I am kinder and more respectful to others. Recently, I saw a quote by Steven Spielberg that brought this perspective back again:

> *I never felt comfortable with myself, because I was never part of the majority. I always felt awkward and shy and on the outside of the momentum of my friends' lives.*

I remember one time when I went to teach a program on personal effectiveness. I pulled into the parking lot and parked next to a VW bus covered with flowers and bumper stickers. Half an hour later, as I was setting up the room, the obvious owner of the VW walked in—a big guy with a long ponytail, bandana, cut-out sweatshirt, and soiled jeans. Thinking he was lost, I asked if I could help. "Yes. Are you Paul? Well, I go by 'Barbed Wire,' and I'm here to be fixed."

Long story short, Charles was a welder in a factory and had a reputation for being difficult—hence

Barbed Wire. Once he had the reputation, he didn't know how to get beyond it. Charles sat through the class, didn't say anything, but participated in all the exercises and seemed to have fun with the other participants, mostly young people from an insurance company. A week later, Barbed Wire's supervisor called and thanked me. It seems he went back to the factory, apologized for being difficult, asked to be called by his given name, and asked to start fresh. Now, I don't think he had some eureka moment in class. Charles simply wanted a fresh start, and the class gave him permission to ask for it.

Charles also taught me a lesson I have relearned many times: don't make up stuff about people based on how they look. We are all appearance biased to some degree. That's why we love people watching— our minds make up stories about people we don't know based on their appearance. It's just the way our minds work. We simply need to remember that what we think initially about others is often not true.

Here are the key points to keep in mind to be great with people—even when they're being difficult.

People are great. This is the only perspective that works out in the long run. We were raised to think there are good people and bad people; that is not useful as a supervisor. Everyone is difficult at times, including you and me.

It's not intentional. People do not stay up all night figuring out how to ruin your day. I know it can seem that way, but they don't. People can be difficult and cause upset, but it's not usually on purpose.

People are complex. Most of us seem to believe we can figure people out—that we can explain why people do the things they do. We can't. But we can learn to be effective with whatever they bring to the conversation.

People's lives are complicated. We can think we know a person's past or current reality. Nope, no way. We do not know what anyone has experienced in their lives nor what they are dealing with from the last twenty-four hours. Not knowing is a good place to start. Trust that people are doing the best they can given their current reality.

Everyone wants to belong. People want to be included, consulted, and informed. No one wants to be on the outside or to have no voice.

People want to contribute. We all want to add value in some way—to our families, colleagues, neighborhoods, and organizations. When we are not sure if we do, our resilience to life's problems is lessened.

Everyone gets defensive when threatened. Here is the most profound idea I have for you with respect to understanding people: people do exactly what makes sense to them in the moment. I'll use a baseball analogy because I love the sport. Think about hitting a baseball. There is no time to analyze a pitch and decide to swing. All major league hitters swing first and then stop the swing if it is not a good pitch. Notice how many checked swings there are—lots. Now think about the difference between a batting-practice fastball and a game-time fastball. One looks hittable, and the other can actually look like a threat if it's too far inside.

When people feel good about themselves, their lives, and circumstances, they usually do the right thing. They tend to be at their best.

When people feel threatened, they often get defensive and do things that are not consistent with being at their best. They take things personally, say things they don't mean, and blame others or justify their behavior— anything to deal with the threat they feel.

So where does this leave you? It may feel uncomfortable, but it's actually a wonderful place. If you start with the perspective that people are great and that they are reacting to the moment, you realize they are in part reacting to you. And you can be safe and catchable or you can be a threat—like a high-and-tight fastball that makes people duck.

How can you be safe? By slowing down, always having time, listening far longer than you might want to, and not trying to fix anyone or their thinking. Just be there—home with the lights on—and realize that if anyone can make a difference with this person, it is you, right now.

The Compassionate Move
Think about who might be feeling disenfranchised or left out right now. Who would really appreciate you checking in with them?

You do not know what wars are going on down there where the spirit meets the bone.
—MILLER WILLIAMS, AMERICAN POET

→ **DO YOU HAVE TIME FOR A CUP OF COFFEE?**

Ashlee, a young project leader, and her colleague Mary Pat were talking on the factory floor about dealing with the constant, almost overwhelming demands on their time.

"When Dave had this job, it wasn't this chaotic," Mary Pat said. "He would be having a cup of coffee with someone now instead of being out here on the factory floor."

Ashlee looked at her as if she were nuts and asked how a cup of coffee would make things less chaotic.

"Dave knew when and with whom he needed to be building relationships to avoid the chaos and indecision."

What Dave's method reveals is that he believed in conversation as the foundation for relationships and that it's essential to work on your relationships before you need to tap into them.

No conversations, no relationships.

Inviting someone to coffee is an invitation to connection and mutual understanding and support. It can also create a safe space in which to have a difficult conversation.

Appreciation: Always Important, Often Missing

I believe that "please" and "thank you" are still the "magic words." But I think the words "I believe in you" may be the most magical of all.

—JODI HILLS, *BELIEVE*

Where do you keep those notes? The ones from a boss or child or colleague—the ones you reread when you need a lift. The notes that when you come across them cause you to slow down for a moment and reflect. The notes that reconnect you with the people who wrote them or to special moments in your life.

It makes a difference to people's experience of

work when they are acknowledged and appreciated. Everyone wants to belong, be liked, and know they make a difference. Yet many people aren't sure what we think of them because we don't tell them often enough.

Remember, You Matter to People

Reflect on each of these questions and consider how you might show appreciation for each person who comes to mind.

→ Who would like more time with you?

→ Who looks up to you?

→ For whom are you a role model?

→ Who notices when you don't say hello?

→ Who have you disappointed lately?

→ Who would be honored by an invitation to a walk or a cup of coffee?

In addition, think about each of your employees or colleagues for a moment. What do you appreciate about them? What do you rely on them for? What might you acknowledge them for? Even better, list ten things you appreciate about each of your employees.

Just the process of writing these down will change your interactions, and you'll find ways to let them know what you appreciate about who they are and what they do.

Handwritten Notes Are Special

Of course, verbal acknowledgment, texts, and email are sometimes the best tools for acknowledging others. They are certainly easy, quick, and comfortable.

Still, personal handwritten notes are one of the most powerful ways to support people. Because handwritten notes are scarce, people respond more deeply to them. They also last as long as people keep them—sometimes years. Each note you write enhances a person's self-worth.

Not comfortable writing notes of appreciation? Here are some examples to get you started:

Thanks for being you. I always feel better when you are involved. Somehow I know that everything will get done. Your dedication and effort are always so evident.

I appreciate what you bring to our group. There is a level of professionalism and integrity that you provide that the rest of us look to and attempt to match.

I sincerely appreciate having the opportunity to work with you. Your calmness makes it easy to handle the stressful work that we do. Plus, I truly respect you as a person and the way you approach life.

I just want you to know that I appreciate your directness. Sometimes it makes the rest of us uncomfortable, but it always moves our conversations along. Without your willingness to say what the rest of us are thinking, we would often not make progress. I also know that you have the interests of everyone in mind.

Thanks for the work you did on the project. It was thorough and accurate. In addition, I want to acknowledge the support and encouragement you consistently provided to everyone else. I know we all appreciated it.

Give yourself three months to not only get good at writing notes but comfortable doing it. Buy some nice note paper and keep it close by. At least once each week, write a note to someone in your life. Make it a note worth keeping. You will feel better, and so will the person who receives your gift.

The Compassionate Move

Don't wait for someone's actions to be above and beyond. Sometimes simply showing up deserves recognition. What everyday actions can you acknowledge?

Every Conversation Can Be Enhanced

> **Each person's life is lived as a series of conversations.**
> —DEBORAH TANNEN, *YOU JUST DON'T UNDERSTAND*

We can all identify decisions we made about ourselves early in life based on what we were told or what was said in our presence. You can most likely recall a conversation with someone—a boss, a parent, a friend—that helped determine who you are today.

Day in and day out, we don't pay much attention to our conversations, but they're what shape our view of the world.

You raise your kids with conversation. If you simply

take the negative comments out of your interactions with them, you will be a different family.

Knowledge, passion, and drive will not set you apart in an organization. Your ability to convene a group of people and make progress during and after the meeting will. After mastering your core discipline and expertise, your ability to influence others is based on your ability to lead and participate in meetings.

Relationships are built and maintained with conversations. Said differently, the quality of any relationship is determined by the quality of your conversations—both speaking and listening.

Think about the last few conversations you had with each person who works for you. What did you talk about? How much candor, openness, and respect were present? If it's not what you want, know you can always improve your conversation and therefore your relationship.

> ## The conversation is the relationship.
> **—DAVID WHYTE, ENGLISH POET**

If you embrace the importance of conversation, then you can focus on noticing what it takes to make every conversation better. These are the fundamental practices for effective conversation: *being present, listening wholeheartedly*, and *being responsible for what you say and how you say it*. Each of these is at the heart of people thinking we care about them.

Be Present

Have you had the experience of being with someone who seems to put the rest of the world on hold while they speak to you? Someone who is genuinely interested in your story and willing to take the time for you to tell it? In a world of distraction, busyness, and multitasking, attention is fleeting, so when you are present and attentive in the moment, those around you notice.

Listen Wholeheartedly

One of the most influential articles I've read was from American journalist Brenda Ueland's book *Strength to Your Sword Arm*. It described what magical things happen when someone is speaking in the presence of a person who knows how to listen without interruption—someone who listens wholeheartedly and then, when needed, adds the supportive request, *"Tell me more."*

Of course, there are times when good conversation is a back-and-forth affair, even a bit chaotic. However, underlying those conversations is the notion of being able to slow down and just listen. So often, that's all people need—to be heard, to feel heard. People are willing to be expressive and vulnerable if they sense that you are truly listening.

Michael Nichols, author of *The Lost Art of Listening*, tells us that *reassuring someone isn't listening. Trying to solve the problem isn't listening. Just listening is listening.*

Yet we don't listen very often, at least not in a way that is meaningful. We interrupt. We finish other people's sentences. We pretend to listen. And people notice.

Attention and caring are tightly connected. If you set aside other work, turn away from your technology, and devote yourself to those speaking, they will take it as a sign that you are interested—that you care.

Be Responsible for What You Say and How You Say It

Consider this point of view: you are responsible not only for what you say but for how it is received. No one expects this of you, but it is a high standard you can set for yourself. Reflect on these questions to help identify where you might improve:

→ What conversations do people associate with you?

→ Do you lean toward speaking first or listening?

→ Do people feel you are truly interested in them?

Or think about mistakes that might detract from someone's experience of being with you:

→ Hijacking every conversation and having it be about you

→ Speaking more often or longer than people can tolerate

→ Making negative comments about someone who is not present

The goal is to speak and listen in a way that people look forward to talking with you.

Four Cs to Look For

Effective conversations have four elements: **clarity**, **candor**, **commitment**, and **completion**. A conversation may seem fine, but you later discover the intended actions or the expected alignment did not occur. When a conversation does not have the desired result, one of these pieces is likely missing.

Check for clarity. Lack of clarity is responsible for many misunderstandings and mistakes. Clarity provides the basis for alignment. Don't assume you have it. Check often by asking, "Is everyone clear?" or "Anyone need more explanation?" If you are not sure, paraphrase what someone said and ask if you got it right or if they have more to say.

Speak with candor. Candor means being authentic—saying what you mean and meaning what you say. A colleague shared the story of a senior manager who always brings his people together for a "no secrets" meeting whenever he conducts facility visits. He wants to know how people are doing, how projects are progressing, and what people need in terms of support and resources. Each of these questions is put into play:

→ What would you like to ask me?

→ What do you think I need to know?

→ Where are you struggling?

→ What are you proud of?

Great questions, but even greater because this manager's invitation to a "no secrets" conversation signals that people have permission to ask and share anything. Of course, it helps that this manager is sincere, authentic, and caring, which creates the trust and safety this kind of conversation requires.

Ask for specific commitments. If you ask for a commitment to be completed by a specific date, it is much more likely to happen than if the action is simply added to someone's list of things to do. People are more productive when facing deadlines. Still, supervisors often don't ask for this kind of specific commitment because they think it might be interpreted as micromanaging or a lack of trust.

One of the keys to project management is being specific about what will be done, when it will be done, and who will do it. I use the expression *X by Y or call*. You're asking someone to do task X by date Y and, if something gets in the way of fulfilling that commitment, to agree in advance to pick up the phone and call you.

Check for completion. This means not changing topics until everyone is ready to move on. This ensures that no critical point or question is left unexpressed. "Do you have anything else to say or ask about this?" "I'm ready to change topics; are you OK with that?" Checking to see if people have anything else to say will reveal issues they might have kept silent about—and that might interfere with clarity and alignment.

Day in and day out, most people simply don't think about their conversations. Consider that every conversation can be enhanced—sometimes with more careful listening, sometimes by removing distractions, sometimes by inviting new voices into the conversation. You can add value to each conversation in which you participate and therefore to every person you touch each day.

The Compassionate Move

At the end of the day, reflect on your conversations—what you said and how you said it. What do you think the other person took away from the conversation? Is it what you intended?

Each conversation we have with our coworkers, customers, significant others, and children either enhances those relationships, flatlines them, or takes them down. Given this, what words and level of attention do you wish to bring to your conversations with the people most important to you?

—SUSAN SCOTT, *FIERCE CONVERSATIONS*

→ WHAT IF YOU LISTEN FLAT-OUT FOR FOUR MINUTES?

Checking in with people is something we've lost in the world of technological connections. Principle #2 covered not walking by people without acknowledging their presence, but this is different. This is purposely interacting with people to develop a relationship and give them a chance to talk.

The topic doesn't matter. Some people will want to talk about their projects or what they have on their schedule for the week. Some will want to talk sports or kids or movies. Taking a few moments to ask about someone's weekend or their latest trip or a project can do wonders, and it doesn't take that long. People can say a lot in four minutes. All you need to do is invite them to share and then pay full attention to what they say. Then you can thank them and excuse yourself. The breakthrough is in realizing you do not need to take twenty minutes. Expressing interest for four minutes will do it.

Say the Right Thing at the Right Time

The final proof of greatness lies in being able to endure [criticism] without resentment.

—ELBERT HUBBARD, AMERICAN WRITER

During my second stint as a supervisor, I had a boss who pulled his direct reports together each month and told us what he thought about our performance. I always left feeling deflated and defeated. One of my colleagues always left the same meeting with a smile on his face, so I asked him for help.

"Paul, quit defending yourself or trying to explain everything you do to Tom. Just nod or say OK. He'll move on; then you can too."

I didn't get it at the time, and my urge to correct my boss's thinking didn't help our relationship.

Later, I discovered what my colleague was saying while watching a movie. It involved a teenager dealing with her father's criticism. She offered no resistance, because if she did, it just wound him up.

I often get unsolicited feedback when I lead workshops. Usually, the feedback is about how it would be better if I did X, Y, or Z. I don't know about you, but I'm not always open to feedback, especially if it feels like criticism. Still, I don't want to be dismissive or arrogant, because people generally have good intentions. So I respond just like the teen in the movie: "Thank you. I appreciate being told."

Done sincerely, it always works.

It's genuine. I mean it. And it doesn't mean I agree with what has been said. It means that I heard it—I got it.

As we covered in the previous chapter, three broad ideas are important to being effective with conversation: being present, listening wholeheartedly, and being responsible for what you say and how you say it. This chapter looks at the last element and offers some specific ways to respond to situations you encounter as a supervisor or colleague.

Reflect on some of your recent interactions and consider whether some of these responses might have been useful.

What would you like from me in this conversation? (*clarifying outcomes and expectations*). When people come to you to talk, ask them up front about what they would like to accomplish.

Thank you. I appreciate being told (*responding to criticism*). Acknowledging that you've heard what was said doesn't mean you agree with it. Explaining or justifying why you did something can appear defensive.

Please say a bit more about what you are asking (*seeking clarity before you respond*). This provides more background for the question and ensures your answer will be relevant. It also gives you a moment to pause before you respond.

May I tell you something? (*asking for permission*). This prepares people to hear what you have to say and makes your tone of voice supportive. Otherwise, you are likely to catch people off guard.

Tell me more or **What else?** (*encouraging the speaker*). You show your interest in people when you ask for more. Instead of jumping in with your thoughts, see where they might take the conversation.

Where are you with this? (*asking for input*). Giving people a chance to express whatever might be on their minds is a key step in achieving alignment. People prefer to be aligned, and if they are not, they will usually tell you why if you ask.

While I would have preferred a different approach, I'll fully support this (*choosing to align*). It's easy to back an idea that matches your own preferences. Part of being a great supervisor is the ability to get behind ideas or decisions that are not your first choice.

I have a request (*asking for action*). This is how

commitments are initiated. Requests are critical to getting things done.

By when will you do that? (*nailing down actions*). Asking for a specific commitment in time is an essential practice in project management.

I'd be willing to do this for you (*offering support*). When you are committed to everyone being successful, you make offers—sometimes outside your traditional roles and responsibilities. You simply do whatever it takes.

Seems like you have an issue with Josh; have you spoken to him yet? (*holding someone responsible for gossip*). Supporting people who are not present is a piece of integrity, and it takes courage.

Did I answer your question? (*checking for completion*). It's easy to misinterpret someone's question or not answer the question fully. Checking back is both gracious and powerful.

I think I'm clear about your idea, and I see it differently. May I tell you? (*disagreeing without* *making someone wrong).* This phrase tends to take the right/wrong experience out of a conversation. It both changes your tone of voice and makes it easier for someone to listen to your view.

Anything else? *(wrapping up a conversation).* This is checking one last time for comments. It ensures everyone is ready to move on.

OK, got it. I'm clear *(letting people know you heard and understood).* This closes the conversation loop and adds clarity and a sense of completion.

The Compassionate Move

Focus for the next week on how you reply to people's comments. Slow down, take your time, and be thoughtful. Practice the above responses. Anything new can feel awkward at first, so use your own words if that helps. Then notice what happens.

The real art of conversation is not only to say the right thing at the right place but to leave unsaid the wrong thing at the tempting moment.

—LADY DOROTHY NEVILL, ENGLISH WRITER

Be Great with Complaints

When you're explaining, you're losing.

—JOSEPH FINDER, *THE SWITCH*

I vividly remember a conversation with my daughter, Amy. I had just come into the house, and she didn't say anything—not like her. In fact, she left the room without a word. I followed her through the house, and finally, she stopped.

"Amy, what's going on?"

"I hate you."

Wow. Some would say I'd finally made it as a parent—having a child tell you she hates you and surviving.

At this point, I quickly reminded myself of what I teach about dealing with people who are upset:

→ **Look past how they express themselves.** People who are upset are rarely gracious, kind, or thoughtful. Don't turn their words or tone into a new problem.

→ **Whatever you resist will persist.** This comes straight out of the martial arts. Go with a blow to lessen its impact. Explaining is resisting.

→ **Don't change the conversation.** Just work to understand what's going on.

→ **Stay with the conversation** until you get to the facts.

→ **Trust yourself and the other person and the conversation.** If you do and stay with it, the conversation always turns out.

So I simply reflected back what Amy said. I didn't alter what she said or resist it.

"You hate me?"

"Well, you are so stupid!"

"I'm stupid?"

"Well, you do stupid things."

"OK, what did I do?"

"You promised to call me, and you didn't."

Ah, the facts at last. I knew what happened, and I knew how to repair the damage. I couldn't do much about *hate* or *stupid*, because they didn't happen.

"OK. You are right. I did promise to call, and I didn't. I apologize. Now how can I make this right?"

Complaints Bring Up Problems You Can Deal With

At times, life stops working the way we want it to. Each of us has had complaints about a supervisor, our colleagues, or even family members. Good people complain. Loyal people complain. Committed people complain.

In fact, people who are willing to speak up about something that is not working for them are a gift to the organization. If you aren't aware of a problem, you can't do anything to resolve it.

You want to handle complaints in a way that both addresses the issue and leaves people feeling good about speaking up. If they aren't complaining to you, they're likely grumbling to one another or keeping quiet out of hopelessness or apathy—and those alternatives are worse.

Behind Every Complaint Is a Request

The task is to hear people out, then ask what they want. What is the request at the heart of the issue they're complaining about? What will resolve it? Here are some examples

Complaint: *Nothing happened as a result of the last employee survey. You say you want our input, but it doesn't seem as if the survey changes anything.*

Underlying request: *We would like to know the process for working with the results of the survey and get a specific list of actions you intend to take as a result.*

If people can clearly state a concern and what they feel will resolve it, you can begin to address the issue. The ability to listen and respond to complaints is a critical skill for supervisors—actually, for anyone!

The Process in Action

Let me share a simple protocol that works for my wife and me when dealing with the complaints that come up at home. It goes something like this:

Cindy: "Paul, I have something I need to talk about" or "We need to talk."

Paul: (I am only allowed one response.) "OK, when you are ready to talk about it, I'm ready to listen." (I don't get to say, "I've got a couple of problems myself" or "How long have you been holding onto this problem?")

Usually, she is ready to talk, so then it's her job to say everything she's concerned about. And while she talks, I simply get to listen. I don't get to be defensive. I don't get to explain my side of it. I simply listen and say, "OK, I get that. What else?" until she says, "That's it."

Now, you might think it's my turn, but it's not. I'm only allowed the next step in the process: "What's your request?"

It's her responsibility to identify what would handle her complaint. Often, she just says, "I just needed to tell you." Other times, she might say, "I request that we talk about that in the future before you do that again" or "I request you don't do that."

This simple but effective protocol helps work through complaints without drama or judgment, and it works equally well with colleagues and direct reports.

If you think about it, most of the problems people have with one another are actually complaints. For example, you can probably think of times when your supervisor or a member of your team did something that didn't work for you, and you were frustrated, maybe even offended, by their demeanor. If you can express your concern clearly and work through it as soon as possible (and not let it fester), then it can be addressed before it becomes a larger issue. It's often a matter of deciding to pay now by having that difficult conversation in a timely manner rather than pay a lot more later after the concern has grown or the parties have dug in their heels.

The Compassionate Move

Listen for hints that people might have a complaint. Pay attention to whatever people say, no matter how indirect, and encourage them to say more about it. Be supportive, even if the complaint seems unfounded or petty.

There's no use talking about the problem unless you talk about the solution.

—BETTY WILLIAMS, IRISH NOBEL LAUREATE

→ USE THESE STEPS TO HANDLE COMPLAINTS.

1. Manager: *Thank you for bringing this issue to my attention. Tell me your concerns.*

2. Employee with complaint expresses the concern fully.

3. Manager just listens, asking questions only for clarity and understanding, then asks: *Is there anything else?*

4. Once the complaint has been expressed and understood, the manager asks the employee: *What will resolve this for you?* or *What is your request?*

5. Employee then asks for what he or she wants: *Please do this* or *I just needed to express this. Thanks for listening to me.*

6. Manager accepts the request or makes counteroffers until they reach agreement.

7. Employee acknowledges manager: *Thanks for supporting me.*

Ask for What You Want, Not What You Think You Can Get

> Learn to ask for what you want. The worst people can do is not give you what you ask for, which is precisely where you were before you asked.
>
> —PETER MCWILLIAMS, AMERICAN WRITER

Most people confuse wishing, wanting, and hinting with action. I had two experiences within about ten days of each other that gave me one of the best ideas for project execution, working with others, and making life work.

I was on an airplane—window seat—on a three-hour flight. When the service cart came to our row, the flight attendant asked me first. I requested a Coke and got a glass full of ice and a few ounces of soda. The woman next to me asked for a glass of ice, a whole can of Coke, a black coffee, and extra cookies. In addition, she asked the flight attendant if he would check back with her later for a refill on the coffee. He said, "Sure."

Wow. I had never thought of asking for the whole can. Instead, I asked for what was comfortable to ask for—what I thought I could get. The woman next to me showed a better way.

Then, the next week, a senior business leader was visiting our factory. Vince was all business and a bit intimidating. He asked me to give him a plant tour, and along the way, we had this conversation:

"Paul, do you have any ideas for improving things in your departments?"

"Yes, I've got several ideas."

"Well, why haven't I seen any capital project requests from you?"

"I guess because I didn't think they would be approved."

"You will never know unless you ask."

The next week, I sent in a request for $7,000 to improve a pumping system. Several days later, I received two copies of my request. The first was covered in red comments with this note at the bottom: "You can do better. You need to be clear, concise, and factual. Improve your writing." The second copy came with no comments—just his signature and the approval stamp.

Making specific requests is at the heart of project management and supervising others. Ask a lot of your people. They want to contribute—to add value to the group. Let them know they can negotiate with you about conditions of satisfaction and completion dates and ask for what they need to accept the request.

A request is "I request that you do thing X by time Y." Including a completion date gives it a better chance of being completed. These are possible options in reply:

→ **Decline**: *I'm going to say no, but let's keep talking so we figure out how to make this work for you.*

→ **Accept**: *I'm willing to do what you ask, and I'll call if I cannot deliver as promised.*

→ **Counteroffer**: *Can we negotiate the date? If so, I'll commit.*

→ **Conditional response**: *I'll accept on this condition.*

→ **Promise to respond**: *Let me look at my schedule, and I'll get back to you this afternoon.*

Establishing a culture that relies on the exchange and completion of specific commitments is part of supervising. To make this process more comfortable and bring everyone on board, consider asking your group to read the *Harvard Business Review* article "Promise-Based Management: The Essence of Execution," which outlines the process and explains the benefits: increased collaboration, agility, and engagement. Then ask for their input on implementing a system of promises and requests.

The Compassionate Move

Think about what you can ask for to keep projects moving, and encourage your employees to ask for what they need to be successful.

People who ask confidently get more than those who are hesitant and uncertain. When you've figured out what you want to ask for, do it with certainty, boldness, and confidence.

—JACK CANFIELD, AMERICAN AUTHOR

If You Give Your Word, Keep It

Every time you give your word, you're putting your honor on the line.

—FRANK SONNENBERG, *FOLLOW YOUR CONSCIENCE*

Ever leave a meeting wondering what, if anything, will happen as a result of it? Ever surprised that people come to a meeting and report they did not complete the actions they agreed upon in the last meeting?

Ever commit to do something and then, as the date gets closer, wish you could be let off the hook for completing it on time?

Ever wish you could call and check on something but worry about being seen as micromanaging?

Ever assign a task to someone because that is the one team member you rely upon when something must get done?

Of course. We have all had these types of experiences.

Giving and keeping your word in our hectic, over-whelmed, excuse-filled world isn't easy. Therefore, if you keep your word every time, simply because you gave it, you will stand out. Most people keep their word depending on who they give it to, whether they got enough sleep, or whether they feel like it.

I feel strongly about this. I grew up in South Dakota. My family used to go fishing in northern Minnesota every summer, and one summer, when I was about eight, it was just Dad and me. As we packed the car, Dad asked, "You want to go to your first baseball game?"

I said, "Wow, that'd be awesome!" So we went to the Minnesota Twins game on a Friday night. At about the seventh inning, Dad turned to me and said, "Have you seen enough? Can we go?"

"No," I said. "I want to stay till the end!"

"OK, we will stay till the end."

The game went into extra innings. We were there until two o'clock in the morning. Not one time did Dad turn to me and say, "We need to leave."

That's who Dad was. If he said he would do something, it was a done deal.

Be Reliable

Imagine what work would be like if this were the most we could ever get from someone: "I'll be there if I can, but don't count on it." Being seen as reliable is an important part of reputation. Effective supervisors model this—and expect their team members to take these actions:

▶ Be specific in what they say they will do.

▶ Include a completion date.

▶ Call and renegotiate when a commitment is in jeopardy.

▶ Provide updates on progress if asked.

▶ Keep a list of everything they have promised.

▶ Offer no excuses for nonperformance.

None of the following are commitments: *I'll look into it. Sounds like a good idea. I'll give it my best. Let me check with my team. OK, let me see what I can do.* These are expressions that well-intended people use when they agree with what is being asked of them but execution is at risk because completion dates are missing.

What Is Your Say/Do Ratio?

What's required to create a culture of reliability is a clear system for the creation, exchange, and completion of actions. Keep track of what percentage of times you keep your word as promised. That is your say/do ratio.

In my experience as a project manager, most teams

finish 60 percent of assigned action items between meetings. High-performing teams average 85 percent. I have a colleague who recommends setting your personal target at 98 percent, because being reliable is so important that you want to give yourself little room to fail.

The other 2 percent. Sometimes life gets in the way. Even the best of us occasionally find that a shift in priority occurs and a task is either not going to be completed as planned or not on time. When that happens, immediately call and discuss the situation with the person to whom you are committed. Together, you can decide the best option:

▶ Stick with the original date.

▶ Change the date.

▶ Revoke the commitment.

▶ Find an alternative way to get the task completed as originally determined.

The Compassionate Move

Follow up with people so they complete their commitments on time. Far better to check in before the deadline approaches and see if they need help than to deal with nonperformance after the deadline has passed.

Commitment is our unique human power to stand up against the whims of fate and circumstance.

–LEWIS B. SMEDES, AMERICAN AUTHOR AND TEACHER

→ EFFECTIVE PEOPLE SAY NO.

Once you decide to complete your commitments on time, you'll realize that saying yes to everything doesn't work. In fact, every time you say yes, you are saying no to something else in life. Also, let your people know they can say no to you. If they can't say no, you can't really count on their yes.

What Do You Think? A Simple Question and Some Common Mistakes

> The spirit wants only that there be flying. As for who happens to do it, in that he has only a passing interest.
>
> **—RAINER MARIA RILKE, AUSTRIAN POET**

While leading a workshop at an Oregon university, an international student asked me a question. "Mr. Axtell, why is it that in this country, everyone asks you how you are doing, yet no one seems to care?"

Supervisors make a similar mistake when they ask their groups for input. One of the most common complaints about supervisors is that they ask for input, then either don't listen to the reply, don't do anything with it, or fail to report back what they did as a result.

Employees want to contribute. If we are committed to engaging each of our team members and gaining their thinking, the question to make that happen is *What do you think?* Depending on the situation, you might ask in various ways:

→ *Here is what I am thinking about for goals this year. Reactions? Concerns? Ideas?*

→ *Let's talk about the experience of working remotely. I'm interested in anything and everything you've got to say about it.*

→ *I'm thinking about filling this position. Questions, thoughts?*

Avoid two other common mistakes:

1. Waiting too long before bringing an issue or decision to the group. The longer you wait, the less

open you are to input. Ask early, before you've got it all worked out in your own mind.

2 Holding back your own views to avoid overly influencing the discussion. If you choose to hold back, give your group permission to ask about your position at any time. In fact, they might want you to go first.

How you conclude a conversation where you have asked for input goes a long way in honoring people and their contributions to a discussion. Consider these options.

Here's what I'm taking away from our conversation (*expressing value*). Take notes and do this wrap-up thoroughly.

I'm not going to do anything with this. Is that OK? (*avoiding expectations*). People leave conversations expecting that you will do something simply because it was discussed. If you don't want this to happen, clarify what you will or will not do as you wrap up the conversation.

I am going to change my mind (*acknowledging value received*). People don't say this very often, and it's powerful when they do—especially when acknowledging they do so as a result of someone's contribution to the discussion. Confident leaders are interested in what works, not whose idea it is.

Here is the process going forward (*being transparent*). Let people know what will happen next and when you will get back to them on what you intend to implement. Give them permission to follow up in case you forget.

The Compassionate Move

Every so often, add a topic to your meetings that engages your group in learning. Enter the conversation without an answer, allowing the wisdom of the group to emerge. For example:

▸ Is there a connection between integrity and courage?

▸ What is our reputation as a group?

▸ What makes the most difference in improving our say/ do ratio?

His questions were very good, and if you tried to answer them intelligently, you found yourself saying excellent things that you did not know you knew, and that you had not, in fact, known before. He had "educed" them from you by his questions...they brought things out of you, they made your mind produce its own explicit ideas...the results were sometimes quite unexpected.

—THOMAS MERTON, *THE SEVEN STOREY MOUNTAIN*

Lead Meetings Like a Pro

> When you go to meetings or auditions and you fail to prepare, prepare to fail. It's simple but true.
>
> —PAULA ABDUL, AMERICAN SINGER

Leadership is a conversational phenomenon. Respected leaders listen in a patient, attentive way and speak in a way that has impact. They use the conversations in every meeting to propel key initiatives, reinforce the cultural values, and develop their people. Given the amount of time they spend in meetings, they recognize the value in mastering the art of leading meetings.

Meetings aren't *just* about delivering results,

although moving projects forward contributes to everyone's success. There are two other outcomes compassionate leaders pay attention to:

 Design and lead meetings with purpose so you honor the time and talent in the room.

② Create a quality experience for each participant.

I was leading a four-day workshop in South America for a Fortune 500 leadership team. At one point, they asked for advice on how to conduct their monthly virtual meetings, since they were only in the same room twice a year. I suggested they conduct an in-person meeting while I observed. Afterward, I told them that they had no chance virtually, because they were not effective when they were in the same room. Everyone laughed, because they knew it was true. People checked their devices, had side conversations, did other work, got defensive, interrupted, strayed away from the agenda, and ended conversations without alignment or actions clearly identified. Now this was a good group, led by a talented executive. Still, without guidelines for effective group conversations, they were lost.

What's my point? You are not alone if you have not yet mastered leading effective meetings. Yet if we include one-on-one meetings, a supervisor spends a significant percentage of time leading or attending meetings, so it pays to be competent in group conversations. The increase in people working remotely makes it even more important.

What follows are key highlights from my other Ignite Reads book, *Make Meetings Matter*, and its follow-up, *Make Virtual Meetings Matter* (available at simpletruths.com).

Design and Lead Your Meetings with a Clear Sense of Purpose

If you were conducting a meeting with the CEO in attendance, you would probably be extra thoughtful about what was on the agenda and how each topic would be discussed. If you call a meeting, it's important that you respect the time of everyone you invite. Only talk about what matters and invite only those directly involved or impacted by the topics. Avoid spending too much time on information sharing. You can use the Basic Structure of a Conversation graphic as a guide to design discussions for each item on the agenda. Process steps for a variety of meeting designs are available for download at paulaxtell.com.

Ask for what you need to lead the meeting. Ask the group for permission to deliberately manage the discussion, and establish agreements at the start. Give it some thought, and ask for whatever help or permission you need to make the meeting work for everyone. For example:

The Basic Structure of a Conversation:

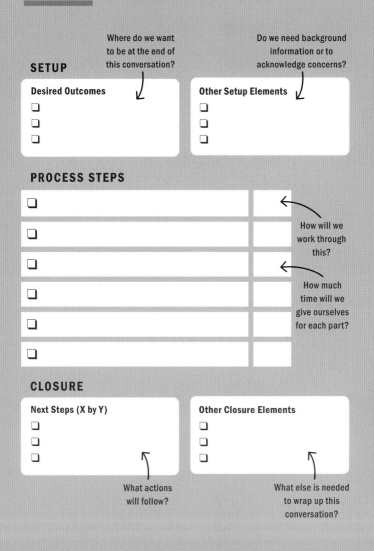

SETUP

Where do we want to be at the end of this conversation?

Do we need background information or to acknowledge concerns?

Desired Outcomes
- ☐
- ☐
- ☐

Other Setup Elements
- ☐
- ☐
- ☐

PROCESS STEPS

- ☐
- ☐
- ☐
- ☐
- ☐
- ☐

How will we work through this?

How much time will we give ourselves for each part?

CLOSURE

Next Steps (X by Y)
- ☐
- ☐
- ☐

What actions will follow?

Other Closure Elements
- ☐
- ☐
- ☐

What else is needed to wrap up this conversation?

→ Ask people to set aside any technology not essential to the discussions.

→ Make full attention and respectful listening the norm.

→ Ask for help keeping the conversation on track.

→ Ask for permission to call on people to broaden participation.

Set up, manage, and close each conversation.
For each topic on the agenda:

→ Set up the conversation. This is about introducing each agenda topic so everyone starts at the same place, is clear about what the conversation is intended to achieve, and how it will get there (the process).

→ Keep the conversation on track. This is the single most important element to more efficient meetings, and it's simple. Train yourself to notice when a conversation begins that is not about the agenda topic or that will not take the group to the desired outcomes.

→ Close each conversation deliberately. This is what ensures that a conversation leads to action and progress. There are five steps:

 Check for completion: *Are there any other questions or comments about this?*

 Check for alignment: *Is everyone agreed on where we ended up on this topic?*

 Confirm commitments: *Who is going to do what by when?*

 Identify and express value: *What are you taking away from this conversation?*

Express appreciation: *Is there anyone we should acknowledge?*

Create a Quality Experience for Every Participant

A quality experience leaves employees feeling more connected, valued, and fulfilled. Here's what I've seen leaders do to create that level of experience.

Work hard to be present. Take adequate time to prepare so you can be available and attentive before and during the meeting. Preparation allows you to relax about leading the meeting and pay more attention to noticing how people are doing as they walk in and throughout the meeting. People associate attention with caring. Observe, listen, ask thoughtful questions, and avoid distractions and multitasking.

Slow the conversation to include everyone. This means fewer agenda items and more time allocated to each topic. Target putting 20 percent fewer items on your agenda and allowing 20 percent more time for each item.

A more inclusive style of conversation means people are likely to notice who hasn't yet spoken and invite them in. To fully implement this practice, call on people gently and strategically. By *gently*, I mean make it feel and sound like an invitation—not some method of controlling participation. By *strategically*, I mean plan for who needs to be part of each discussion topic. Ask yourself:

→ Who would be great at starting the conversation?

→ Who is impacted by the outcome?

→ Who is most likely to have a different view?

→ Who are the more experienced people who might sense whether we are making a mistake or missing something?

Check in with people. Begin and end each meeting with this question: *Does anyone have anything to say or ask?* Ask it deliberately and with a tone that signals this conversation matters to you—and then wait. Pausing conveys that you're not interested in getting to someplace other than right here, right now—that this conversation matters.

Ensure progress between meetings. Two things will lead to more productivity between meetings: a timely meeting summary and follow-up on action items.

A written summary keeps the conversation alive. A single page will suffice for most meetings. The intent is to capture key points and the specific commitments made for each topic so people who didn't attend—and those who did—will have a record of who will take further action.

Follow up. Good people sometimes do not keep their word. They take work home. They are on too many teams. They say yes when they should say no. Most people are busier than they want to be and have more on their plate than they can handle. Follow-up isn't micromanaging or a lack of trust. Checking with people is not only good project management, it's also an act of support.

The Compassionate Move

Be responsible for each person's experience of being in the meeting. With this mindset, you will notice opportunities to be supportive and appreciative—and to have people truly look forward to your meetings.

Great meetings don't just happen—they're designed. Producing a great meeting is a lot like producing a great product. You don't just build it. You think about it, plan it, and design it.

—MICHAEL BEGEMAN, AMERICAN EXECUTIVE

Building a Powerful Group, One Relationship at a Time

> **I don't like that man. I must get to know him better.**
> **—ABRAHAM LINCOLN, AMERICAN PRESIDENT**

As an engineer, I love designing ways to make things happen with ease. I like to design systems and processes and structures—from chemical processes and meetings to decks and bonsai trees. It's about bringing order, simplicity, and elegance to various parts of life.

This includes designing conversations to create relationships and trust among teams and between supervisors and employees. I love these two questions to start such conversations:

→ *What can I tell you about myself that will make it easier to understand me and work with me?*

→ *Is there anything at all about which you are curious, wondering, anxious, or concerned?*

The first is a question I learned at a team-building workshop at the Pecos River Learning Center. It is designed to create a conversation where we can learn more about one another, which leads to new levels of trust and respect.

The second question comes from Tim Gallwey's book, *The Inner Game of Work.* Tim had this insight that any time we are not at our best, there is simply a thought that is in the way. He then invented the question to use in clearing away those background thoughts.

I often put these two questions together when asking senior managers to do a question-and-answer session with employees. First the manager speaks for eight minutes, answering the first question. Then the

→ **TRY AN EXERCISE IN GETTING TO KNOW ONE ANOTHER.**

This is adapted from the oral history project StoryCorps, but instead of putting people face-to-face, do a "story walk." According to author and humanitarian activist Jacqueline Novogratz, "We found that when you let the air blow around people, magic can sometimes happen."

The idea is to walk outside with each other for forty minutes. For the first ten minutes, one person talks and tells his or her story, then the other person asks questions for the next ten minutes. Then you change roles and repeat the process on the way back.

manager asks Gallwey's clearing question, and the group determines where the conversation goes by asking questions.

I remember doing this for the top ranger of a national park and her employees. It was the first time that many of the employees had a chance to relax with the ranger and just talk. The conversation was wide ranging, sometimes emotional, and refreshingly direct. As people finally realized they could say and ask anything and get an honest, genuine answer, the questions became more compelling and worthwhile.

Finally, after about an hour, one staff member said, "We've been whining and complaining and expressing our frustrations for this entire session. It's been all about us. What can we do to make your job easier?"

The top ranger paused, then said, "One thing: please give me the benefit of the doubt. If I make a decision, it's always after losing sleep over it and thinking about it long and hard. You can always question what I do, but I'd like you to be on my side and know my heart is always in the right place. That would be great if you'd do that."

This wide-open, employee-driven Q&A may seem risky, but in my experience, people respond to your willingness to be open and trust them by being engaged and respectful. If we can trust ourselves, one another, and the conversation, it almost always turns out.

Agreements Give Powerful Groups Freedom

That brings me to another conversation to have with your team—one about agreements. The park ranger's request was for an agreement.

Many problems can be avoided with a few simple agreements. They're the basis for special relationships.

Agreements aren't hard-and-fast rules but guidelines put in place to clarify how to work together and to reduce the frequency and severity of problems. Our lives work to the extent to which we keep our promises and agreements with one another, so be thoughtful about what you put in place.

Here is a basic set of agreements for a supervisor and a group, written from the supervisor's viewpoint. You can modify these to fit your own experience and needs:

→ *Let's be clear about goals and expectations. If anyone is not sure, let's sit down and discuss until we have clarity and agreement.*

→ *You can ask me anything at all about working for me or this organization, and I'll tell you the truth.*

→ *If I have any concern about your performance or hear any concerns from the organization about you, I will tell you within one week.*

→ *Let's agree on how we will be in communication throughout the week.*

→ *I promise to be on your side and support you completely.*

Here is a set of basic team agreements that you can build upon with more of your own.

→ *We will say what we are thinking as honestly and respectfully as we can.*

→ *We will listen generously to each person and respect their views.*

→ *If we commit to doing something, we will do it as promised or let someone know if there's a problem.*

→ *We will acknowledge and appreciate one another.*

→ *We will have one another's backs.*

→ *If we have a problem with anyone, we will let them know directly.*

How will you know when you have a powerful group? People will want to join your team because your team cares about people and wants everyone to succeed.

The Compassionate Move

Schedule a conversation in one of your upcoming meetings to clear the decks. Ask the question from the beginning of this chapter: *Is there anything at all about which you are curious, wondering, anxious, or concerned?*

To me, teamwork is a lot like being part of a family. It comes with obligations, entanglements, headaches, and quarrels. But the rewards are worth the cost. With a combination of practice and belief, the most ordinary team is capable of extraordinary things.

—PAT SUMMITT, AMERICAN BASKETBALL COACH

A Simple Coaching Process—Shift from Telling to Asking

Listening connects us and heals the hurt we carry—we can make a world of difference for one another by listening.

—PATTY WIPFLER, AMERICAN AUTHOR

One aspect of caring is being able to help someone sort out a problem. If you can listen for ten minutes and then ask questions that might lead to clarity and a path forward, you can make a difference to anyone who walks into your office.

When a person brings a problem to you, the first instinct is to default to solving the problem and providing answers based on your own experience.

The better move is usually to help employees think through the problem themselves, and that's essentially a matter of asking questions and listening. Besides, this coaching approach saves you time while developing the skills of your employees.

Let me give you two simple examples. First, let's say you come to me because you want to improve your performance. I agree and ask you to call me once a week for the next eight weeks. In addition, I ask you to tell me what three questions I should ask you each week. You might respond:

→ *How am I doing about getting out of here by 5 p.m.?*

→ *How can I be a better colleague?*

→ *How can I improve the meetings I lead?*

Then each week, you call, and I ask you to speak about each of the questions. Afterward, you tell me what you intend to do in the next week to maintain momentum on each issue.

That's the process. Your performance will improve because you know what you need to do, and discussing it keeps it in front of you. Awareness leads to change.

Second, let's say you have a particular issue you've been losing sleep over and not making progress on. Perhaps you are overwhelmed by work or aren't getting started on a project. Again, we schedule a regular conversation, and I ask a series of questions:

→ *What have you done about this so far?*
→ *What are you thinking now about the issue? Say everything that comes to mind.*
→ *What is the next best thing for you to do about this?*
→ *When will you do that?*

Then, for accountability, I'll ask you to send me a text or email when it's completed.

Part of being a supervisor involves setting direction and giving advice, especially to new employees.

More often, though, it's important to shift from telling to asking questions and listening.

The following template gives you a straightforward approach to most issues that people might bring to you. Of course, it's important to put it into your own words and use the parts that work for you in any given conversation. You can follow it exactly and it will work, but tailor it to fit you and your group.

Here are additional questions to use in specific situations.

Questions for solving a problem:

→ *Where do you want to be at the end of this conversation?*

→ *What is the worst that can happen? Can you live with that?*

→ *What are you committed to that makes this a problem?*

→ *What becomes possible if you do this?*

→ *What are you waiting for?*

Simple Coaching Process:

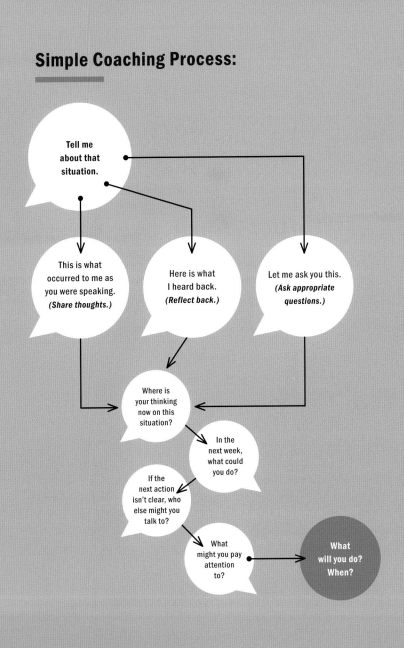

Questions for improving performance:

→ *What is everything you need to accomplish in the next three weeks?*

→ *What would a remarkable week look like?*

→ *Are you are spending your time on the right things?*

→ *What three things, if completed, would give you a sense of fulfillment for the week?*

Questions for looking forward:

→ *What might you accomplish in the next hundred days?*

→ *What would you like to be true in the future that is not true now?*

→ *If you made a list of twenty-five things you want in life, what would be on your list?*

→ *How can you maintain momentum on each of your projects?*

The Compassionate Move

Catch yourself giving advice this week, and see if you can ask questions instead.

Coaching is unlocking a person's potential to maximize their own performance. It is helping them to learn rather than teaching them.

—SIR JOHN WHITMORE, *COACHING FOR PERFORMANCE*

Good Supervisors Have Problems—Lots of Them

Find the courage to ask questions
and to express what you really want.
Communicate with others as clearly as
you can to avoid misunderstandings,
sadness, and drama. With just
this one agreement, you can
completely transform your life.

—MIGUEL ÁNGEL RUIZ, *THE FOUR AGREEMENTS*

Why do good supervisors have problems? Because good supervisors care, and if you care, you are going to have problems.

I remember attending a class on parenting when

my kids, Jesse and Amy, were in junior high school. One of the discussions that stayed with me was about problems. It resonated with the entire group of parents when the workshop leader said:

→ *Good kids have problems.*

→ *Good parents have problems.*

→ *Life is a series of problems.*

A sigh of relief went through the room as all of us got some freedom from thinking that perhaps we weren't good parents or there was something wrong with our kids. What a gift to be reminded that life is a series of problems for everyone.

Create an Empowering Mindset about Problems

Most of us were raised thinking that good people didn't have problems, so having problems meant you were somehow bad or unsuccessful. If you reflect on this notion, however, it just doesn't make sense. Life is a never-ending stream of problems, especially if you manage people.

So embrace this perspective: *If you care, you are going to have problems.*

It's easy to be a supportive parent when your child brings home straight As. The challenge is to be supportive and safe and kind when you see Ds.

It's the same with being a supervisor: you've got to be great even when major customers are lost, assembly lines go down, or quality problems occur. Focus on these elements.

Listen deeply. If you make time, listen deeply, and treat what people say with respect, people will tell you what they need to tell you. React in a way that adds to your reputation rather than diminishes it. When people are vulnerable, they need to know you are on their side.

Be consistent. If you take some things in stride but fly into a rage at others, your people will be left walking on eggshells and checking with one another to gauge what kind of mood you are in—and that won't work out well.

Look past how they communicate when they are upset. You want people to give you bad news and let you know when they are upset. Drama happens. None of us were trained to be gracious and kind and gentle when we're upset. Two ideas have helped me immensely: (a) give up your right to be offended, and don't offend, and (b) be calm and calming.

No one wants to look bad. No one wants to disappoint management. Everyone is concerned when problems happen on their watch. In fact, the concern about what people will think is often worse than the problem itself. Make sure you are not someone people worry about. Focus on the solution and avoid blaming anyone.

Be genuine. Sincerity means everything. Be yourself. Be down-to-earth. Be a good person who strives to do the right thing. People will respond.

Be truthful. Being truthful with people when they make mistakes is a must. Just speak respectfully and supportively. Let people know as soon as you have any concern at all about their actions. Don't wait until it becomes a big deal.

Vulnerability Is a Strength

Leadership is a dance where sometimes you need to take the lead and go first. People who are willing to be vulnerable give others permission to show their own vulnerability. It's not about being weak or at risk. It is about revealing yourself—your weaknesses, your worries, your thinking. Consider the following as powerful expressions:

→ *I'm not myself today. I'm a bit overwhelmed with preparing for senior management's visit on Friday.*

→ *Just so you know, I'm dealing with a personal issue and may seem distracted until I get it resolved. Nothing to worry about, but I'm clearly not myself.*

Sharing that you have problems makes you real—someone people can relate to. It's not that you have to share all your troubles with your group; rather, if you have a current issue affecting your interactions, it is often worth sharing. It also demonstrates that you would be willing to hear what's going on in their situation.

Rely on Yourself

When the world keeps telling us that problems are bad and good people don't have problems, it can be challenging to keep a positive mindset. I keep a card on my desk as a reminder that I'm the one who can make a difference. This is what it says:

Life is problems. Having problems is a part of being committed. I am up to challenges. I want to make a difference. People are important to me. I care. Therefore, I am going to have problems. It's supposed to be like this. Now, what is the next best move for me with this dragon?

The Compassionate Move

When a problem occurs, find a way to pause before you react. Count to ten. Walk around the block. Wait to respond until you get some distance and perspective, then choose a response you will not regret later, one that meets your values and standards for being in the world.

Everything will be all right in
the end. If it's not all right,
then it's not yet the end.

—DEV PATEL, *THE BEST EXOTIC MARIGOLD HOTEL*

Take Care of Yourself So You Can Be There for Others

When you cease to fear your solitude, a new creativity awakens within you.

—JOHN O'DONOHUE, IRISH POET

You first! Being there for your people ultimately begins with finding time for yourself. It's difficult to demonstrate compassion and caring when you are fighting your own demons.

One of my favorite work experiences was being a shift supervisor on a new facility start-up in Seattle. In particular, I loved the night shift because there was always more time to hang out with the operating personnel—and to hang out with myself.

I know managers who look forward to working in their gardens or taking long walks with their dogs each weekend. Others like to get up early before the house wakes up. Some prefer to go into the workplace in the off hours when no one is there.

Two important aspects of self-care require time alone. First, time to decompress is essential to sorting out life, finding clarity, and relaxing in the face of difficult or stressful circumstances. Second, finding time for critical thinking about current situations or future plans is an important aspect of being an effective supervisor.

Yet in a busy, distracted, technology-driven world, we often forget what critical or creative thinking even looks like.

At one point in my life, I felt I had lost my creativity. I just didn't seem to have ideas or dreams or any sense of looking forward in my life. Then something happened. I was training to run a marathon, and about an hour into a long run, my Walkman died. (Yes, it was a long time ago.) I needed music both to get me started on my runs and to keep me going. But suddenly the Pointer Sisters and Dwight Yoakam were gone.

Then something amazing happened: my mind shifted gears and started *using* the time it had just been given. My creative self was back. It had simply been crowded out by being busy and distracted with background music and other noise.

As you plan your week, think about what you need to be at your best. Taking care of yourself first might be exactly what would allow you to be available for others. Here are some key ideas.

Find time alone. Shoot for three two-hour blocks each week. Doing nothing would be fine. Doing something you love would be great. Starting a project that you've been putting off for ages also works. Stepping away from your daily grind is both refreshing and recharging.

Set aside technology at least once a day. Maybe it's just for twenty minutes, but it would be great if you can make it two hours. While we don't want to be without technology, just the presence of any device interferes with our ability to be present. Let's break the mindless habit of checking devices and consciously choose when to use them.

Start doing only one thing at a time. It's a myth that multitasking is effective. When you multitask, you are simply doing two things poorly. Just as a stop sign doesn't read "kinda-sorta" stop or safety programs don't intend for you to be "kinda-sorta" safe, if you are multitasking, you are kinda-sorta present.

Cut back on your open-door policy, the practice of being available to anyone, at any time, for anything. Certain tasks can't be accomplished unless you make time to focus exclusively on them. Imagine what you might accomplish if you could dive deep into an issue or draft your outline for a presentation. Uninterrupted time alone to decompress, to think strategically, and to work on key initiatives is just as important as being available. Find a quiet spot where no one can find you a couple of times a week.

Turn your car radio off. What challenges do you

need time to think through? What issues have been nagging for your attention? If you turn the radio off during your commute, your mind will either solve a problem or start working on the future. Keep a list of things you want to sort out on your next car ride or walk.

Develop your ability to think out loud. Once in a while, you need velocity in developing an idea, formulating a plan, or reacting to circumstances. There is something about thinking out loud with another person that leads you to clarity and solutions more quickly. Find someone who knows how to listen, and see what happens when you can just talk.

Be open to being coached. You can accomplish more in life if you do not work alone. Being coached, taking lessons, or asking for help does not in any way diminish who you are. These are the basic ideas:

→ *You cannot watch yourself perform.* Asking someone to observe you and provide feedback always leads to insights.

→ *You are better when you are being watched.* Just the idea of having someone observe you increases your attention to performing well.

→ *Take lessons from a pro.* Deliberate practice is part of learning. Working with an expert helps you know what good practice looks like.

→ *Surround yourself with people who are better than you.* Rather than comparing and judging your own performance, be curious about how others do it so well.

Read. Fiction is best. Reading is an escape from the rest of the world. Books with strong characters foster empathy. Ten articles from the *New York Times* each month will expand your worldview and broaden your thinking. Start with thirty minutes a week, and work your way up to two books a month.

Always be learning something. Your mind loves to learn, especially things that are difficult to master. It's why people love golf and kids love video games. Learning something difficult also gives the mental toughness to respond to mistakes in a positive way. That, in turn, will make you kinder and calmer with others who are learning or struggling.

The Compassionate Move

Being truly attentive and empathetic with your people begins with compassion for yourself. Find at least two hours three times this week to decompress. Turn the radio off when you drive or go for walks, and notice how your mind uses the time.

Be a good steward of your gifts. Protect your time. Feed your inner life. Avoid too much noise. Read good books, have good sentences in your ears. Be by yourself as often as you can. Walk. Take the phone off the hook. Work regular hours.

—JANE KENYON, AMERICAN POET

Conclusion

Caring and working with others in a compassionate way is a journey worth pursuing. If you choose to embark on this journey, there will probably not be a final station at the end, but there will be many wonderful stops and moments along the way.

We were all raised differently. Some of us were raised to be quiet, gentle, and kind. Some of us were raised to compete and outperform. We are exactly as we should be given our past experiences. The question for each of us is who do we want to be going forward?

Of course, there isn't a single answer. It depends on your circumstances and your role. Each of your kids might see you in a different way. Each of your employees might need something different in their relationship with you.

My hope is this book has given you the principles to guide you toward being who you want to be at work and perhaps other places too!

Finish every day and be done with it. You have done what you could. Some blunders and absurdities no doubt crept in. Forget them as fast as you can. Tomorrow is a new day; begin it well and serenely, with too high a spirit to be cumbered with your old nonsense.

—RALPH WALDO EMERSON, AMERICAN ESSAYIST

Recommended Reading

→ *Distracted: The Erosion of Attention and the Coming Dark Age* by Maggie Jackson

→ *Deep Work: Rules for Focused Success in a Distracted World* by Cal Newport

→ *Great Leaders Have No Rules: Contrarian Leadership Principles to Transform Your Team and Business* by Kevin Kruse

→ *Talent Is Overrated: What Really Separates World-Class Performers from Everybody Else* by Geoff Colvin

→ *Fierce Conversations: Achieving Success at Work & in Life, One Conversation at a Time* by Susan Scott

→ *Drive: The Surprising Truth About What Motivates Us* by Daniel Pink

→ *Radical Candor: How to Get What You Want by Saying What You Mean* by Kim Scott

→ *The Shallows: What the Internet Is Doing to Our Brains* by Nicholas Carr

→ *The Inner Game of Work: Focus, Learning, Pleasure, and Mobility in the Workplace* by Timothy Gallwey

→ *Dare to Lead: Brave Work. Tough Conversations. Whole Hearts.* by Brené Brown

→ *The Infinite Game* by Simon Sinek

Acknowledgments

This book is another example of Scott Adams's quote that goals don't make things happen, systems do. Without Erin McClary at Sourcebooks championing the idea, Cheryl McLean at Jackson Creek Press holding the space to write and rewrite it, Cheri Boline finding everything we had written something about some time long in the past, and Cindy making room for me to check out while writing, this book doesn't happen.

In addition, for every supervisor and manager who has asked me a question over the last thirty-five years, I'm grateful. For me, thinking and writing only occur when someone asks me a question that I've not considered before. This also includes hundreds of people who want desperately to have a wonderful relationship with their supervisor and are not sure how to start.

About the Author

PHOTO © CINDY OFFICER

Paul Axtell provides consulting and personal and group effectiveness training to corporations, universities, and nonprofit organizations. With an engineering degree from South Dakota School of Mines and an MBA from Washington University in St. Louis, Paul's early career was spent in manufacturing, engineering, and management.

For the last twenty years, Paul has been devoted to designing and leading programs that enhance individual and group performance, whether for line workers and admin staff at a manufacturing plant or regional managers and CEOs in global corporations. His decades of insights led to a succinct collection of fifteen strategies in *Being Remarkable*, the small but powerful centerpiece of the Being Remarkable series training program.

Paul's second edition of *10 Powerful Things to Say to Your Kids: Creating the Relationship You Want with the Most Important People in Your Life* applies these concepts to the special relationship between parents and children of all ages. Named Best Parenting Book by several award programs, it has been translated into Korean, Vietnamese, Chinese, Arabic, French, and Spanish and is now available in audiobook format.

The award-winning *Meetings Matter: 8 Powerful Strategies for Remarkable Conversations* offers a deep dive into improving meeting competence and is the foundation for *Make Meetings Matter* and *Make Virtual Meetings Matter.*

Paul lives with his wife, Cindy, in Phoenix.

NEW! Only from Simple Truths®

IGNITE READS
spark impact in just one hour

IGNITE READS IS A NEW SERIES OF 1-HOUR READS WRITTEN BY WORLD-RENOWNED EXPERTS!

These captivating books will help you become the best version of yourself, allowing for new opportunities in your personal and professional life. Accelerate your career and expand your knowledge with these powerful books written on today's hottest ideas.

TRENDING BUSINESS AND PERSONAL GROWTH TOPICS

 Read in an hour or less

 Leading experts and authors

 Bold design and captivating content